Meat-eating Dinosaurs

Robin Birch

CHELSEA CLUBHOUSE
An Imprint of Chelsea House Publishers

Chelsea Clubhouse
An imprint of Chelsea House Publishers
132 West 31st Street
New York, NY 10001

Chelsea Clubhouse books are available at special discounts when purchased in bulk quantities for businesses, associations, institutions, or sales promotions. Please call our Special Sales Department in New York at (212) 967-8800 or (800) 322-8755.

You can find Chelsea Clubhouse on the World Wide Web at: http://www.chelseahouse.com

First published in 2002 by
MACMILLAN EDUCATION AUSTRALIA PTY LTD
15–19 Claremont Street, South Yarra, 3141

Visit our Web site at www.macmillan.com.au or go directly to www.macmillanlibrary.com.au

Associated companies and representatives throughout the world.

Library of Congress Cataloging-in-Publication Data
Birch, Robin.
  Meat-eating dinosaurs / by Robin Birch.
  p. cm. — (Dinosaur world)
  Includes index.
  Summary: Describes the appearance, eating habits, and habitat of meat-eating dinosaurs, including Tyrannosaurus, Deinonychus, Compsognathus, Gallimimus, and Baryonyx.
  ISBN 978-1-60413-407-0
  1. Dinosaurs—Juvenile literature. 2. Predatory animals—Juvenile literature.
  [1. Dinosaurs. 2. Predatory animals.] I. Title. II. Series.
  QE861.5 .B57 2009
  567.912—dc21

                                                                    2008000842

Edited by Angelique Campbell-Muir
Illustrations by Nina Sanadze
Page layout by Nina Sanadze

Printed in the United States of America

Acknowledgements
Department of Library Services, American Museum of Natural History (neg. no. 6744), p. 16; Auscape/ Francois Gohier, pp. 5, 12; The Field Museum (neg. no. GEO85818c), p. 7 (bottom); © The Natural History Museum, London, pp. 20, 25, 28; Royal Tyrrell Museum of Palaeontology/Alberta Community Development, p. 7 (top); Southern Images/Silkstone, p. 8.

While every care has been taken to trace and acknowledge copyright, the publisher tenders their apologies for any accidental infringement where copyright has proved untraceable.

Contents

Glossary words

When a word is printed in **bold**, you can look up its meaning in the Glossary on page 31.

Dinosaurs

Dinosaurs lived millions of years ago. There are no dinosaurs alive today.

There were many different kinds of dinosaurs.

We know dinosaurs lived because scientists have dug up and studied their bones.

These bones belonged to a meat-eating dinosaur.

Meat-eaters

Some dinosaurs ate animals and others ate plants. The dinosaurs that ate animals are called meat-eaters.

Some meat-eating dinosaurs were huge and some were small.

Huge meat-eaters ate other dinosaurs. Small meat-eaters ate insects and other small animals. Most meat-eating dinosaurs had sharp teeth for catching and chewing their food. We can see their sharp teeth in their **skulls**.

The sharp teeth in these skulls show that they belonged to meat-eating dinosaurs.

Meat-eating dinosaurs had scales on their skin, as all other dinosaurs did. Snakes, lizards, and other **reptiles** that live today have scales on their skin, too.

scale

This reptile skin has scales on it.

Meat-eating dinosaurs lived both in forests and in places with few trees. They lived wherever there was food to be caught.

Meat-eating dinosaurs hunted in forests.

Tyrannosaurus

(tie-RAN-uh-SAWR-uhs)

Tyrannosaurus was one of the biggest meat-eating dinosaurs. It was as heavy as an elephant and stood about 20 feet (6 meters) tall.

large teeth

two fingers

Tyrannosaurus had three toes with strong claws on each foot. It had two fingers on each of its small arms. Each finger had a sharp claw.

Tyrannosaurus was a large, heavy dinosaur.

Tyrannosaurus had a huge head with strong **jaws** up to 4 feet (1.2 meters) long. It had as many as 60 long, sharp teeth that it used for grabbing and cutting food. When a tooth fell out, another one grew in its place.

Tyrannosaurus had long, sharp teeth.

Tyrannosaurus used only its mouth and feet to catch its **prey**. Its arms were too short to grab animals. Tyrannosaurus could eat up to 500 pounds (230 kilograms) of food in one bite.

Tyrannosaurus used its teeth to pull its prey apart.

Deinonychus

(die-NON-ih-kuhs)

Deinonychus was a light, fast-moving, and fierce hunter. Its powerful jaws held many sharp, curved teeth for slicing its food. It had a curved, bendable neck that helped it grab its prey.

sharp curved teeth

14

Deinonychus had a long, **stiff** tail that helped it stay balanced and make fast turns. Its long arms each had three fingers that it used to hold onto its prey.

long stiff tail

Deinonychus was a small but fierce dinosaur.

The skeleton of this dinosaur shows that one claw on each foot was long and curved. Deinonychus could bend this claw back and then swing it down quickly to stab an animal.

long tail for balance

long curved claw

This skeleton of Deinonychus is in the jumping position.

These dinosaurs probably hunted in groups called **packs**. They searched forests and open country for prey. They probably attacked a large dinosaur by jumping on it together to make the kill.

Three Deinonychuses attack an Iguanodon.

Compsognathus

(komp-sog-NAY-thus)

Compsognathus was a tiny dinosaur about the size of a chicken. It could run very fast on its two long, thin legs.

sharp spiky teeth

18

This dinosaur had two clawed fingers on each short arm. It had a long, straight tail that helped it stay balanced when it ran.

long straight tail

long thin legs

Compsognathus was a tiny meat-eating dinosaur.

Compsognathus probably lived in dry areas with low-growing plants. Scientists have found its **skeleton** buried in rock. The skeleton is a **fossil**.

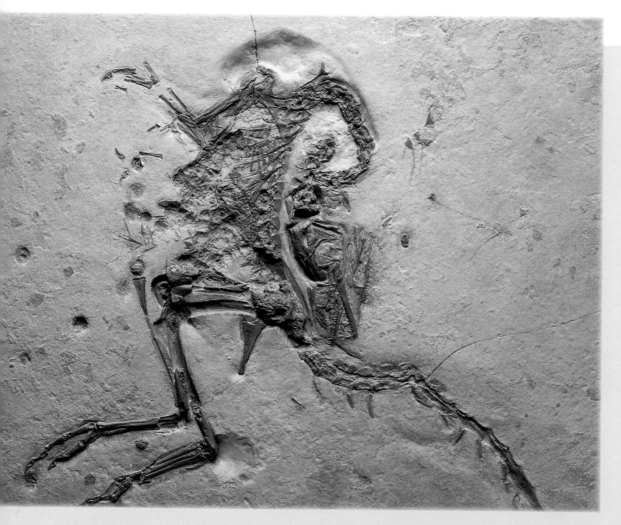

This Compsognathus skeleton is buried in rock.

Compsognathus had a long, narrow head and many sharp, spiky teeth. It probably caught and ate insects, small lizards, and small furry animals the size of mice.

beetle

mammal

mouse

dragonfly

lizard

cicada

Compsognathus probably ate foods such as these.

Gallimimus

(gal-uh-MY-muhs)

Gallimimus was a tall, **slender** dinosaur. It had a long neck for a meat-eater and a long stiff tail. It could hold its head up high to watch for other dinosaurs that might attack.

long stiff tail

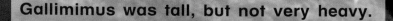

Gallimimus was tall, but not very heavy.

Gallimimus had short arms with three fingers on each hand. It probably used its hands to help catch small animals.

long neck

long thin legs

Gallimimus had long, thin legs, which helped it run very fast. This dinosaur looked like today's ostrich and probably ran like one, too. It lived on dry land and walked along riverbanks to find food.

Gallimimus looked similar to an ostrich.

Gallimimus had a small head and a long, flat beak with no teeth. It probably ate small lizards, large insects, and dinosaur eggs. It swallowed its food whole.

long flat beak

This Gallimimus skeleton shows that it had no teeth.

Baryonyx

(bare-ee-ON-iks)

Baryonyx was a large dinosaur with a long neck and a long, stiff tail. It had a head like a crocodile.

head like a crocodile

large curved claw

Baryonyx had strong, **muscular** legs. Its front legs were only a little shorter than its back legs. Scientists are not sure whether Baryonyx walked on two or four legs.

strong legs

Baryonyx was a large, strong dinosaur.

Many small, pointed teeth filled Baryonyx's narrow jaws. Baryonyx probably lived near rivers where it could find fish to eat. Its long jaws and sharp teeth would have been good for grabbing slippery fish.

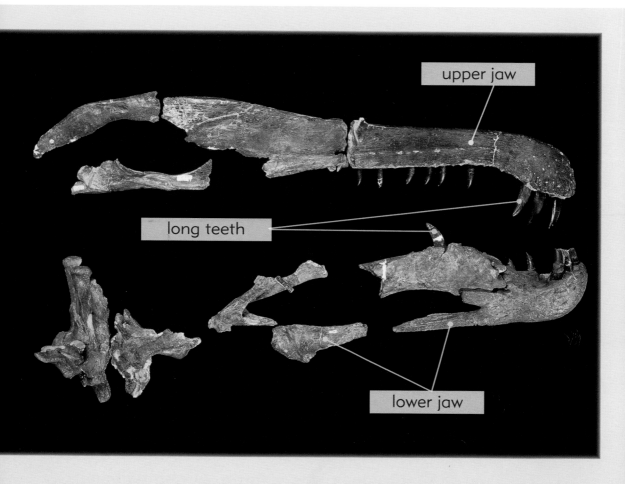

These parts of a Baryonyx skull show some of its long teeth.

Baryonyx had huge curved claws on its hands that were 12 inches (30 centimeters) long. It may have used these claws for lifting fish out of the water. Baryonyx is the only known dinosaur that ate fish.

A Baryonyx catching a fish in a river.

Names and Their Meanings

"Dinosaur" means "terrible lizard."

"Tyrannosaurus" means "**tyrant** lizard."

"Deinonychus" means "terrible claw."

"Compsognathus" means "pretty jaw."

"Gallimimus" means "chicken mimic."

"Baryonyx" means "heavy claw."

Glossary

fossil   something left behind by a plant or animal that has been preserved in the earth; examples are dinosaur bones and footprints.

jaw   the bones in the head that hold teeth

muscular   having large, well-developed muscles

pack   a group of animals that hunt together

prey   an animal that is hunted by other animals for food

reptile   a cold-blooded animal that breathes air through its lungs, lays eggs, and has scales

skeleton   the bones that support and protect an animal's body

skull   the bones of the head

slender   slim or thin

stiff   does not bend

tyrant   a cruel or unjust ruler

Index